THIS JOURNAL
BELONGS TO

....

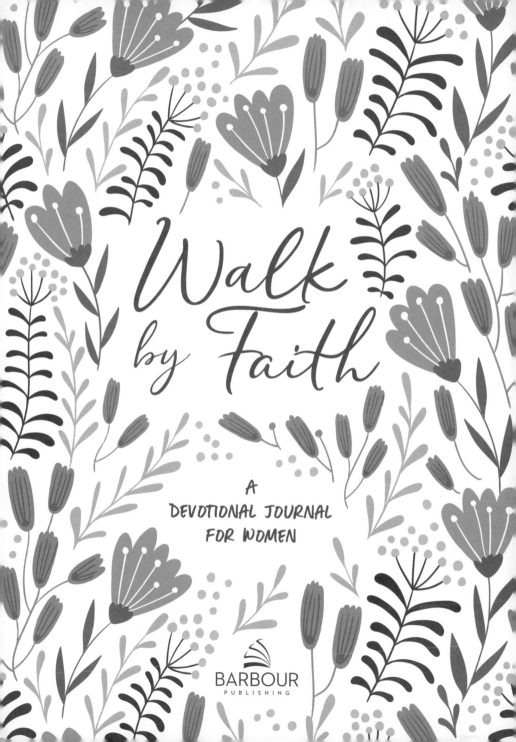

Walk by Faith

A
DEVOTIONAL JOURNAL
FOR WOMEN

BARBOUR
PUBLISHING

INTRODUCTION

The Bible says that "without *faith* it is impossible to please God" (Hebrews 11:6 NIV, emphasis added). God places the importance of faith at the very top of the list, and the reason is simple: Faith is the key by which we gain access to Him. How can we love Him when we aren't sure He exists? How can we trust Him when we aren't sure He wants to be part of our lives? By faith we come into God's presence and establish a relationship with Him.

Walk by Faith was designed to open your eyes to faith—to take it from word to concept to experience. It is our prayer that as you move through these pages, you will hear God's voice calling you to place your faith in Him in every aspect of your life.

- -

Without faith it is impossible to please Him, for he
who comes to God must believe that He is, and that
He is a rewarder of those who diligently seek Him.
HEBREWS 11:6 NKJV

NO BOUNDARIES!

For as high as the heavens are above the earth, so great is his love for those who fear him; as far as the east is from the west, so far has he removed our transgressions from us.
PSALM 103:11–12 NIV

· ·

God's love for us surpasses all boundaries. If we go to the highest highs or the lowest lows, He will meet us there. No matter where we are in our faith journey, He stands with arms wide, ready to forgive our sins. We don't understand this kind of love. Then again, if we could understand it, perhaps it wouldn't feel like such a gift. Thank God for a love that knows no boundaries.

GOOD NEWS FOR THE NATIONS!

This same Good News that came to you is going out all over the world. It is bearing fruit everywhere by changing lives, just as it changed your lives from the day you first heard and understood the truth about God's wonderful grace.

COLOSSIANS 1:6 NLT

The word *gospel* means good news. We have good news for the nations! Jesus Christ came and gave His life for all! If you had great news that affected your children or friends, wouldn't you share it? Of course you would. The same holds true with the nations. When we develop a love for the rest of the world (and this is God's heart for us all as believers), we can't help but share the good news.

COURAGEOUS FOOTSTEPS

*"Blessed is she who has believed that the Lord
would fulfill his promises to her!"*
LUKE 1:45 NIV

In Jesus' day, women had fewer opportunities to stretch their wings creatively and professionally than they do today. That didn't stop them from holding tightly to God's promises and stepping out to act on what they believed. You can follow in their courageous footsteps. Whatever you believe God wants you to do—big or small—don't hold back. Today, take at least one step toward your goal. With God's help, you'll accomplish everything He's set out for you to do.

SPIRITUAL LEADER

A wise woman strengthens her family.

PROVERBS 14:1 NCV

Moms wear many hats. They're called to be chefs, teachers, maids, nurses, mediators, and activity directors—sometimes, all at the same time. But God has entrusted you with an even more important role in your family. You're a spiritual leader. As you live out your faith, share the "whys" behind what you do. Point your children in directions that will lead them closer to God. A strong faith helps build a stronger family.

GOD FIRST

"Seek the Kingdom of God above all else, and live
righteously, and he will give you everything you need."
MATTHEW 6:33 NLT

. . . .

Putting God first sounds like the right thing to do. But what does that look like in real life? Does it mean spending every moment reading the Bible or praying over questions like "Paper or plastic?" Holding God's kingdom as your top priority simply means that God's way becomes your way. Each day, ask God to help you live and love in a way that brings Him honor. Then watch Him provide what you need to do what He asks.

ALWAYS WELCOME

Because of Christ and our faith in him, we can now
come boldly and confidently into God's presence.
EPHESIANS 3:12 NLT

Being in the presence of someone you've wronged isn't a comfortable place to be. Even after apologies have been offered and restitution made, a feeling of shame and unworthiness often lingers. This isn't the case in our relationship with God. When we set things straight through faith, all that remains is God's love. Draw close to God in prayer. Never be afraid to enter His presence. You're always welcome, just as you are.

LEARN TODAY

Our Lord, in all generations you have been our home.

Psalm 90:1 cev

Your family's unique. You may be married, single, with kids or without. Parents, siblings, aunts, cousins. . .they're all part of the family God's placed you in. That family can be a testing ground for faith. That's because the more time you spend with people, the easier it is for them to rub you the wrong way—and vice versa. Consider what God wants to teach you through your family. Patience? Forgiveness? Grace? Don't put off until tomorrow what you could learn today.

GOD SUPPLIES

Those who hope in the LORD will renew their strength.
They will soar on wings like eagles; they will run and
not grow weary, they will walk and not be faint.

ISAIAH 40:31 NIV

Every woman has days when she's feeling weary. But sometimes, this feels more like the norm than just a down day. When this happens, welcome weariness as a messenger. It's a reminder you're in need of renewal. Get alone with God and ask, "Is there anything I need to change? What's out of my hands and in Yours alone?" Allow God to do His job. Then through the strength God supplies, do what you can with what you have.

LIKE A SHIELD

Let your faith be like a shield.
EPHESIANS 6:16 CEV

. . . .

Some women keep their faith tucked away like a family heirloom, displaying it only on holidays like Easter and Christmas. But if you truly believe what God says is true, faith will be part of your everyday life. Faith is more than words of comfort. It's a shield that can protect you from an assault of doubt or the temptation to do something you know goes against God's plans for you. Take faith with you wherever you go.

HE DELIVERS

Now faith is confidence in what we hope for and
assurance about what we do not see.
Hebrews 11:1 niv

It's been said that death and taxes are the only things we can be certain of in our lives. The Bible tells us that faith brings its own gift of certainty. Because of God's promises and His faithfulness in keeping them in the past, we have the assurance that He'll come through for us in the future. He's promised we're loved, forgiven, cared for, and destined for heaven. Rest in the fact that what God promises, He delivers.

PERFECTLY

Your kingdom is an everlasting kingdom, and your dominion
endures through all generations. The LORD is trustworthy
in all he promises and faithful in all he does.
PSALM 145:13 NIV

God's faithfulness to you never falters. It began before you were born and will last far beyond the day you die. Nothing you do, or don't do, can adversely affect His love and devotion. This kind of faithfulness can only come from God. Those who love you may promise they'll never let you down, but they're fallible. Just like you. Only God is perfect—and perfectly trustworthy. What He says, He does. Today, tomorrow, always.

INSIDE AND OUT

*GOD met me more than halfway, he freed me from my
anxious fears. Look at him; give him your warmest
smile. Never hide your feelings from him.*

PSALM 34:4–5 MSG

God knows you inside and out. He knows how you feel, right here, right
now. So why bother telling Him what's going on in your heart? Because
that's how relationships grow. Sharing your personal struggles with a
spouse or best friend is a sign of intimacy. It demonstrates your faith in his
or her love for you. It also gives the other person an opportunity to offer
comfort, help, and hope. God desires that same opportunity in your life.

DISCIPLINED BY LOVE

*The Lord disciplines those he loves,
as a father the son he delights in.*

PROVERBS 3:12 NIV

· ·

When we discipline our children, it's because we love them and want the best for them. We're training them to be responsible adults. It is the same with God. He disciplines us out of love because He wants the very best for us. When we strike out on our own, away from His principles and blessings, He has no choice but to reel us back in. Love always disciplines.

CONTROL AND CLARITY

But even if we don't feel at ease, God is greater than our feelings, and he knows everything.

1 JOHN 3:20 CEV

. . . .

Do you regard your emotions as friend or foe? Your answer may depend on how much they control your life. God created humans as emotional beings. Your wide range of emotions—including empathy, anger, compassion, joy, sorrow, and fear—helps you assess situations and decide on appropriate action. But it takes God's wisdom to balance the power of your emotions. When emotions run high, ask God for control and clarity before you act.

DRAW NEAR

I walk in the LORD's presence as I live here on earth!
PSALM 116:9 NLT

· ·

At times, God's presence is elusive. Although you believe in Him, you forget He's there. But He's like the air around you: invisible, yet essential to life. Remind yourself of God's presence each morning as soon as you awake. Breathe in and thank God for His gift of life. Then breathe out, asking Him to make you more aware of His hand at work in your life. Throughout the day, just breathe—drawing near to the one who gave you breath.

IN LINE WITH THE TRUTH

Everything you ask for in prayer will
be yours, if you only have faith.

MARK 11:24 CEV

Faith keeps our prayers in line with the truth behind what we say we believe. If we believe God loves us, believe Jesus is who He said He was, believe God has a plan for our lives, believe He's good, wise, and just—our prayers will reflect these beliefs. They'll be in line with God's will—with what God desires for our life. These are the kind of prayers God assures us He'll answer, in His time and His way.

SECRET INGREDIENT

*This is the secret: Christ lives in you. This gives
you assurance of sharing his glory.*
COLOSSIANS 1:27 NLT

. . . .

When it comes to family recipes, some women remain mum on the secret ingredient that makes their great-grandmother's pot roast, pound cake, or pickled beets stand out from the rest. You have a secret ingredient in your life that assures your future will turn out perfectly. But this secret is meant for sharing: when you put your faith in Jesus, you are assured of spending eternity with Him. Pass it on—and you'll be blessing future generations!

GENEROUS

*All the Lord's followers often met together,
and they shared everything they had.*
ACTS 2:44 CEV

In our culture it's considered admirable to pull yourself up by your own bootstraps—or kitten heel pumps, as the case may be. But God asks His children to walk together, leaning on one another for support. Being generous in sharing our time, our resources, and our experience helps God's family grow stronger as a whole. As we hold on loosely to what we've been given, our arms will be more able to hold on tightly to those around us.

GOD KEEPS HIS COVENANT

"Understand, therefore, that the LORD your God is indeed God. He is the faithful God who keeps his covenant for a thousand generations and lavishes his unfailing love on those who love him and obey his commands."
DEUTERONOMY 7:9 NLT

. . . .

A covenant is an agreement between two parties. Sure, we sign on the dotted line—or shake hands on a matter—but we don't always follow through. Not so with God. He always follows through on His agreement, even when we fall short. And He continues to lavish us with His unfailing love when we love Him and obey His commands.

GOD'S FAMILY

May the God who gives endurance and encouragement
give you the same attitude of mind toward
each other that Christ Jesus had.

ROMANS 15:5 NIV

God's family is like your own biological family. You're bound to get along better with some members than with others. When God paints a picture of unity among His people, it doesn't mean disagreements and misunderstandings disappear. It simply means that the faith you share will encourage you to work through any problems that arise. As a part of God's family, you can learn what love really looks like, encouraging one another toward growth while helping smooth out each other's rough edges.

DRAWN TOWARD JESUS

In your relationships with one another, have the same mindset
as Christ Jesus: Who, being in very nature God, did not consider
equality with God something to be used to his own advantage.
PHILIPPIANS 2:5–6 NIV

Even those who don't believe Jesus is God can agree that He was an
extraordinary person. The way Jesus selflessly loved others, reaching out
to people society cast aside demonstrates an attitude of compassion,
humility, and service. We're drawn to those who sincerely care for us.
That's one reason why we're drawn toward Jesus. Believing in a God who
believes in us doesn't feel risky. It feels like accepting a free invitation to
be unconditionally loved.

DOLLARS

But remember the LORD your God, for it is he who
gives you the ability to produce wealth.
DEUTERONOMY 8:18 NIV

A paycheck comes with a sense of entitlement. You earned it, so you get to choose how to spend it, right? But have you ever stopped to consider how the way God created you impacts your ability to earn a living? Take a moment right now to thank God for His part in your financial picture. Ask Him to give you wisdom, self-control, and a spirit of generosity as you choose how to use every dollar you receive.

EASY TO RECOGNIZE

Be joyful in hope, patient in affliction, faithful in prayer.
ROMANS 12:12 NIV

How do you build a relationship with a friend? You spend time together. You talk about everything, openly sharing your hearts. Prayer is simply talking to your best friend. True, it's harder to understand God's reply than it is to read a friend's text or pick up her phone message. But the more frequently you pray, the easier it is to recognize God's voice. So keep talking. God's listening. With time, you'll learn how to listen in return.

SINGING OF HIS LOVE

I will sing of the LORD's great love forever; with my mouth
I will make your faithfulness known through all generations.
I will declare that your love stands firm forever, that you
have established your faithfulness in heaven itself.
PSALM 89:1–2 NIV

When you're filled with the love of the Lord, it's hard to contain the song that rises in your heart. Why stop it? Let it flow! Praise makes even the hardest situation manageable. And what a great witness! When others hear you humming, when they see your passion for praise, they will wonder what you have that they don't. Join in the greatest love song of all time today—praise to the King of kings!

BECAUSE OF YOU

*When your faith remains strong through many trials,
it will bring you much praise and glory and honor on the
day when Jesus Christ is revealed to the whole world.*

1 PETER 1:7 NLT

. . . .

The thought of God praising you may be a new one. But when Jesus returns, what you've done and overcome because of your faith will be visible to all. But it's not the accolades of others that make this worth anticipating. It's the chance to see God smile—and know it's because of you. In this life, you may feel your efforts go unnoticed. Rejoice in knowing God sees and praises everything you do because of your faith in Him.

JUST WHAT YOU NEED

"No one can serve two masters. . . .
You cannot serve both God and money."
MATTHEW 6:24 NIV

When you were a little girl, what was the "one thing" you wanted? You knew you'd truly be happy if only it were yours. Adults often feel the same way. If only we had more money, this "one thing" could be ours! But when we focus on our wants, we become a slave to those longings. There's only "one thing" that truly satisfies—having faith in the God who loves you enough to provide exactly what you need.

LOVE IS PATIENT

*Love is patient, love is kind. It does not envy, it does not boast,
it is not proud. It does not dishonor others, it is not self-seeking,
it is not easily angered, it keeps no record of wrongs.*

1 Corinthians 13:4–5 niv

• •

Oh, how impatient we are! We want what we want—and we want it now! No waiting. But love isn't impatient. It doesn't demand immediate service. Instead, love waits patiently on the sidelines. The next time you feel yourself losing your patience, take a deep breath. Remind yourself: love holds on for the ride.

A TRUE PARADISE

If we confess our sins to God, he can always be
trusted to forgive us and take our sins away.
1 JOHN 1:9 CEV

Faith and forgiveness are two sides of the same coin. You cannot hold on to one without embracing the other. If you believe that Jesus loves you so much that He would pay the penalty for your sins with His own life, then you must also believe that He wouldn't hold those sins against you any longer. If you're feeling guilty, talk to God. Your feelings are not always truth tellers. God's forgiveness is what makes spending eternity with Him a true paradise.

WHAT GOD REQUIRES

*"And now, Israel, what does the L*ORD *your God require of you, but to fear the L*ORD *your God, to walk in all his ways, to love him, to serve the L*ORD *your God with all your heart and with all your soul?"*

DEUTERONOMY 10:12 ESV

It's fascinating to think that God "requires" us to love Him. More interesting still is that it's listed in this scripture along with walking in His ways, fearing Him, and serving Him. These things work well together, and they are all the better when love is tucked in the middle. First we fear (respect) God; then we show our love by obeying Him; and that leads to a life of service.

IMMEDIATELY. COMPLETELY. ETERNALLY.

*Be even-tempered, content with second
place, quick to forgive an offense.*

Colossians 3:13 msg

. . . .

When you put your faith in God, the very first thing He does is forgive you. He doesn't overlook what you've done. He forgives it. Immediately. Completely. Eternally. Choosing to follow His example isn't always easy. But it's always right. When others offend you, don't let your forgiveness hinge on their apology or repentance. You can wisely set boundaries and still offer forgiveness. Ask God to help you forgive before another's fault can fester into a painful, distracting grudge.

FREE TO BE

*I will walk in freedom, for I have devoted
myself to your commandments.*
PSALM 119:45 NLT

Without rules, what sounds like freedom can be chaos. Take driving, for instance. You need a license to operate a motor vehicle. That's not because the DMV thinks you're an incapable driver. It's because traffic flows more freely when everyone knows and follows the rules. The same is true when living a life of faith. God's commandments help us build stronger relationships. We're freer to be ourselves and to love God and others well when we follow His rules.

KEY TO FREEDOM

*The Scriptures declare that we are all prisoners of sin,
so we receive God's promise of freedom
only by believing in Jesus Christ.*

GALATIANS 3:22 NLT

· ·

Imagine being locked in prison for years. You're guilty, hopeless, helpless. Then a beloved friend volunteers to take your place. You're set free as another woman takes your punishment as her own. How much do you value the cost of your freedom? In essence, this is what Christ did for you. When you place your faith in Him, you're handed the key to freedom. Honor Jesus' gift by living a life worthy of such sacrifice.

RESTART

You're my place of quiet retreat;
I wait for your Word to renew me.

PSALM 119:114 MSG

If your computer has a glitch, it's helpful to refresh the page or reboot the whole program by pushing RESTART. God helps us refresh, reboot, and restart by renewing us through His Spirit. When you're in need of refreshment—even if you've already spent time with God that day reading the Bible, singing His praises, or praying—take time to sit quietly in God's presence. Push RESTART. Wait patiently and expectantly for a word from the one you love.

JOYFUL IN HOPE

Be joyful in hope, patient in affliction, faithful in prayer.
ROMANS 12:12 NIV

Hope is a precious commodity, isn't it? When we're hopeful, we can endure almost anything. It gives us the ability to patiently endure even the toughest of challenges. And hope is also a wonderful companion to love. When you love people, you find yourself treating them with more patience. You're hopeful that the relationships God has blessed you with are going to grow stronger and stronger as time goes by.

KEEP HIS WORD

Jesus answered him, "If anyone loves me, he will keep my word, and my Father will love him, and we will come to him and make our home with him. Whoever does not love me does not keep my words. And the word that you hear is not mine but the Father's who sent me."

JOHN 14:23–24 ESV

Love and obedience have always walked hand in hand. If we love God, we will obey Him. Sure, our flesh doesn't always want to do it, but we'll have the best outcome if we stick with the teachings of the Bible and follow God's precepts to the best of our ability. Love equals obedience.

FAITH THAT WON'T FAIL

*If Christ wasn't raised to life, our message
is worthless, and so is your faith.*
1 Corinthians 15:14 cev

Faith, in and of itself, is nothing more than trust. If you place your trust in something that isn't trustworthy, your faith is futile. You can have faith that money grows on trees, but ultimately that faith isn't going to help you pay your bills. Putting your faith in Jesus is different. Historical and biblical eyewitness accounts back up Jesus' claims. That means putting your faith in Jesus is both logical and powerful. It's a faith that won't fail.

HEART CHANGES

Jesus went to Galilee preaching the Message of God: "Time's up!
God's kingdom is here. Change your life and believe the Message."
MARK 1:14–15 MSG

. . . .

What you believe will influence the choices you make. If you believe in gravity, you won't jump from a seventh-story balcony to save time in getting to your hair appointment. If you believe what Jesus says, you'll change the way you live. Jesus often talks about the importance of traits such as honesty, purity, and generosity. Though God's Spirit helps change your heart, it's the daily choices you make that bring traits like these to maturity.

ANEW

The faithful love of the LORD never ends!
His mercies never cease. Great is his faithfulness;
his mercies begin afresh each morning.
LAMENTATIONS 3:22–23 NLT

We all blow it. We let anger turn our words into weapons. We fall back into patterns we vowed we'd never repeat. We feel ashamed of ourselves as wives, mothers, or friends. But this is another minute, another morning, another chance to begin anew. Faith can break a cycle of regrettable yesterdays—if we let it. God offers forgiveness and a fresh start to all who ask. He never tires of us bringing our brokenness to Him.

ONLY WHAT IS HELPFUL

Do not let any unwholesome talk come out of your mouths,
but only what is helpful for building others up according
to their needs, that it may benefit those who listen.
EPHESIANS 4:29 NIV

Oh, how we love to talk about others. We don't usually set out to gossip or cause pain, but often that's how things end up. We get carried away. We share our "concerns" with others. God longs for us to guard what we say, dwelling only on what is helpful. That's how love operates. It compels us to build others up, not cut them down. May every word be beneficial.

AWAKEN TO LOVE

I will sing of your strength, in the morning
I will sing of your love; for you are my fortress,
my refuge in times of trouble.
PSALM 59:16 NIV

Oh, the love of God! It's such a wonderful gift, pouring down from the throne of God. Realizing His great love for us is overwhelming. We can't help but praise! We find ourselves waking in the morning with songs of worship on our lips, thanking God for all He's done for us. What an awesome way to start the day.

AN INSIDE JOB

We look inside, and what we see is that anyone
united with the Messiah gets a fresh start, is created
new. The old life is gone; a new life emerges!

2 Corinthians 5:17 msg

Faith is the ultimate makeover. But it doesn't hide who you are with a lift or tuck here and a fresh coat of foundation there. This makeover isn't external. It's eternal. And it's totally an inside job. Jesus referred to it as being "born again." Those old habits, regrets, and mistakes are behind you. Your past is forgiven, and your future empowered by God's Spirit working through you. Let go of yesterday and grab hold of God's promise for today!

LIFE LETTER

*These are written so that you will put your faith
in Jesus as the Messiah and the Son of God. If you
have faith in him, you will have true life.*

JOHN 20:31 CEV

The Bible is like a letter from your best friend. In it, God shares how much He loves you, what He's been up to since the creation of the world, and His plans for the future. You're an important part of those plans. The life you live through faith is the letter you write in return. But others will also sneak a peek at your "life letter." The life you live may be the only Bible some people ever read.

SPUR ONE ANOTHER ON

*And let us consider how we may spur one
another on toward love and good deeds.*

HEBREWS 10:24 NIV

Do you have a friend who needs your encouragement? One who needs a real boost? Ask yourself, "How can I spur her on?" "What can I say that will make a difference?" Can you write her a note of encouragement? Speak words of faith regarding her situation? Love spurs us on, and words of kindness from a friend do the same. Take time to build up your friend in love.

LOVE OVERCOMES TIMIDITY

For the Spirit God gave us does not make us timid,
but gives us power, love and self-discipline.
2 Timothy 1:7 niv

Sometimes we're afraid to share our testimony with others or to talk about our faith. We're timid. We hold back. How wonderful to realize that God gave us a spirit of power, love, and self-discipline. With these three things firmly in place, we're able to open up and share the good news of His love.

MAKE TIME

Just as lotions and fragrance give sensual delight,
a sweet friendship refreshes the soul.

PROVERBS 27:9 MSG

. . . .

Jesus' disciples were more than just apprentices learning the ins and outs of faith. They were also Jesus' closest friends. They walked together, talked together, ate together, and prayed together. When Jesus knew His time on earth was short, He turned to them for support. Follow Jesus' example. No matter how busy you get, make time for the friends God brings into your life. They may be God's answers to prayers you're praying today.

AUTHENTIC

Giving an honest answer is a sign of true friendship.
PROVERBS 24:26 CEV

Teenage girls are sometimes known for being petty and cliquish. But you're all grown up now. You're not only a woman; you're a woman of faith. That means it's time to put away childish habits, especially those that keep you from loving others well. A true friend doesn't play games or hide behind masks. She's honest about who she is, open about her strengths, weaknesses, hopes, and fears. Her honesty invites others to be as authentic with her as she is with them.

AN ACT OF HEART

Let love and faithfulness never leave you; bind them around
your neck, write them on the tablet of your heart.
PROVERBS 3:3 NIV

Dogs are known as "man's best friend." That's because dogs are faithful. They don't hold a grudge or get so preoccupied with their own lives they forget to greet you at the door. That kind of loyalty comes easy to a dog. But for complex human beings, it takes an act of will—and heart. With God's help, you can become a woman others can depend on. Including God. Live out your faith by becoming more faithful.

WHOLESOME AND EVERLASTING

*"I chose you. I appointed you to go and produce
lasting fruit, so that the Father will give you
whatever you ask for, using my name."*
JOHN 15:16 NLT

Pick up a banana at the supermarket, forget about it for a few days, and voilà! You wind up with a black, mushy mess. There's only one kind of fruit that doesn't spoil. That's spiritual fruit. Because of your faith in God, you can trust He's growing wholesome, everlasting fruit in you. You can nurture this fruit, helping it grow to maturity by watering it frequently with God's words. Read the Bible. Then watch what God produces in your life.

PROPER CONDITIONS

*The Holy Spirit produces this kind of fruit in our lives: love,
joy, peace, patience, kindness, goodness, faithfulness, gentleness,
and self-control. There is no law against these things!*

GALATIANS 5:22–23 NLT

Fruit doesn't ripen through its own hard work. It doesn't will itself to grow juicier. Fruit just does what it was created to do. It grows into something beautiful and beneficial. God's Spirit is the only one who can bring this spiritual fruit to maturity in you. But you can provide the proper conditions to encourage growth. Have faith that God is at work. Put into practice what you learn. Then have patience. Harvest time is coming!

INTO PRACTICE

Truth, righteousness, peace, faith, and salvation are more than words. Learn how to apply them. You'll need them throughout your life. God's Word is an indispensable weapon.
EPHESIANS 6:14–17 MSG

• •

What you do with God's words is ultimately what you decide to do with God. If you read the Bible for inspiration, without application, your faith will never be more than a heartwarming pastime. While it's true the Bible can be a source of comfort, it's also a source of power and an instrument of change. Invite God's Spirit to imprint the Bible's words into your heart. Then step out in faith and put what you've learned into practice.

LEAPING ACROSS MOUNTAINS

Listen! My beloved! Look! Here he comes, leaping across the mountains, bounding over the hills. My beloved is like a gazelle or a young stag. Look! There he stands behind our wall, gazing through the windows, peering through the lattice.
Song of Songs 2:8–9 niv

. . . .

God's desire is that we enter into an intimate relationship with Him. He runs to us when we're at our lowest point, offering a shoulder to weep on and words to comfort. He longs for us to curl up in His lap and share our heartbreaks. And He celebrates with us when we're having a great day. We are His bride! He cares about everything that affects us. Why? Because He's madly in love with us!

BELIEVING WITHOUT SEEING

Jesus said, "So, you believe because you've seen with your own eyes. Even better blessings are in store for those who believe without seeing."
JOHN 20:29 MSG

If you're shopping for a pair of shoes, you don't rely on a salesperson's description. You want to see them. Try them on. Walk around in them awhile. The same is true when it comes to trying on faith for size. We long to see the one we've chosen to place our faith in. But Jesus says believing without seeing holds its own special reward. Ask Jesus to help you better understand those blessings as you walk in faith today.

ONE STEP AT A TIME

Because Jesus was raised from the dead, we've been given
a brand-new life and have everything to live for,
including a future in heaven—and the future starts now!
1 PETER 1:3–4 MSG

The future isn't something that's waiting off in the distance. It's right here, right now. Every breath you take brings you into that future, one step at a time. And the future that awaits you is good. Faith changes the course of your future as surely as it changes the landscape of your heart. God is preparing a home for you that will never be torn down, a place where your questions will be answered and your longings fulfilled.

WE BELONG TO EACH OTHER

My lover is mine, and I am his.

SONG OF SOLOMON 2:16 NLT

There's something very special about the relationship between an earthly husband and wife. When you're married, you can say, "We belong to each other!" and mean it. The same is true of the relationship between Christ and His bride, the church. We belong to Him, and He belongs to us! We're knit together. Bound by love. Woven together by grace.

HIS LOVE TOWARD US

For great is his love toward us, and the faithfulness
of the LORD endures forever. Praise the LORD.
PSALM 117:2 NIV

. . . .

We'll never be able to understand God's love toward us. It extends
grace when grace is the last thing we deserve. It offers forgiveness when
we've committed the most heinous of sins. It reaches out to us when
we're haughty and proud and comes looking for us when we've sunk to
the lowest low. Doesn't that kind of love make you feel like shouting?
Like praising God at the top of your voice?

WORTH WAITING FOR

*"For I know the plans I have for you," declares
the LORD, "plans to prosper you and not to harm
you, plans to give you hope and a future."*
JEREMIAH 29:11 NIV

For centuries, people have turned to fortune-tellers, crystal balls, and horoscopes in the hope of glimpsing the future. Turning to anything or anyone other than God for this kind of information is futile and forbidden by scripture. It's also unnecessary. God holds our future in His hands. He has a plan and a purpose for what lies ahead. We may not know the details of all our tomorrows, but faith assures us it's worth waiting for.

BIGHEARTED

I am praying that you will put into action the generosity that comes from your faith as you understand and experience all the good things we have in Christ.
PHILEMON 6 NLT

When you choose to follow Christ, your faith opens the floodgates of countless good gifts. You receive things like forgiveness, salvation, a future home in heaven, and God's own Spirit living inside you. God's generosity is incomparable. It can also be motivational. When someone is incredibly generous with you, it inspires you to share more generously with others. Whether it's your time, your finances, your home—or things like forgiveness, grace, or love—follow God's example. Be bighearted and openhanded.

"NOWHERE" BLESSINGS

"Turn to face God so he can wipe away your sins,
pour out showers of blessing to refresh you, and send
you the Messiah he prepared for you, namely, Jesus."
ACTS 3:19–20 MSG

Blessings are gifts straight from God's hand. Some of them are tangible, like the gift of a chance acquaintance leading to a job offer that winds up helping to pay the bills. Some are less concrete. They may come wrapped in things like faith, joy, clarity, and contentment appearing seemingly "out of nowhere" amid difficult circumstances. The more frequently you thank God for His blessings, the more aware you'll be of how many more there are to thank Him for.

A SATISFIED SOUL

Because your love is better than life, my lips will glorify you.
I will praise you as long as I live, and in your name
I will lift up my hands. I will be fully satisfied as with the richest
of foods; with singing lips my mouth will praise you.

PSALM 63:3–5 NIV

Ah, satisfaction! Such a comforting feeling. Did you know that God wants us to be satisfied with His love? Our souls can be satisfied in Him. So what does it mean to be satisfied? It means we're okay with His plan, not ours. We trust in His love for us. He has our best interest at heart. Today, allow the Lord's overwhelming love to satisfy your heart, your mind, and your soul.

EXTENDING LOVE AND PRAYER

"But I tell you, love your enemies and pray
for those who persecute you."
MATTHEW 5:44 NIV

· ·

We usually enjoy praying for others, as long as we're in good relationship with them. But this whole "Pray for your enemies" thing is tough! We don't want to ask God to bless our enemies. If we're honest, we're usually hoping for the opposite! But God commands us to love our enemies and to pray for them too. So who's on your "enemy" list today? Better get busy!

UTMOST LOVE AND CARE

Have you ever come on anything quite like this
extravagant generosity of God, this deep, deep wisdom?
It's way over our heads. We'll never figure it out.

ROMANS 11:33 MSG

Consider what it would be like to own everything. Absolutely everything. Even the universe is under your control. It seems like it would be easy to be generous. After all, you've got so much. But God treasures every speck of His creation—especially His children. Entrusting us with free will and with the job of caring for this planet was a risky venture. Honor God's generosity by treating His gifts with the utmost love and care.

PERSONAL TRAINER

*Give your burdens to the LORD, and he will take care of
you. He will not permit the godly to slip and fall.*
PSALM 55:22 NLT

It's important for us women to do some heavy lifting as we age. Weight-bearing exercise helps keep our bones strong and our muscles toned. But bearing mental and emotional weight is another story. These don't build us up. They break us down. Allow faith to become your personal trainer when it comes to what's weighing heavily on your mind and heart. God knows how much weight you can bear. Invite Him to carry what you cannot.

BE GLAD!

Satisfy us in the morning with your unfailing love,
that we may sing for joy and be glad all our days.
PSALM 90:14 NIV

Can you imagine waking up satisfied every morning? God's unfailing love can cause you to do that. You can wake up with a song on your lips and a joyful heart. Why? Because His love sustains you through the night. It gets you through the dark places. The valleys. You awake to a new day, fresh with His love and His insight. Ah, morning! What a wonderful time to praise!

LOVING THOSE IN NEED

*If anyone has material possessions and sees a
brother or sister in need but has no pity on them,
how can the love of God be in that person?*
1 JOHN 3:17 NIV

If we love God, we need to take care of others even if it means reaching into our wallet to do it. Material possessions are meant to be shared. They're a tool for ministering to others. People see our love when we take pity on them in their need. And when we give, our hearts are exposed. Love comes pouring out.

TOWARD UNCONDITIONAL LOVE

You can develop a healthy, robust community that lives right with God and enjoy its results only if you do the hard work of getting along with each other.

JAMES 3:18 MSG

. . . .

What are your greatest accomplishments? Earning a degree? Landing a big account? Lovingly leading a toddler through the terrible twos? Whatever you've accomplished, hard work undoubtedly played a part in your success. The same goes for relationships. Going beyond superficiality toward unconditional love is hard work. It's a relational journey that takes patience, perseverance, forgiveness, humility, and sacrifice. It's a journey God willingly took to build a relationship with you. Now it's your turn to follow in His relational footsteps.

OUT OF LOVE

If you are having trouble, you should pray.
And if you are feeling good, you should sing praises.
JAMES 5:13 CEV

If you're a mom, you know your children will ask for help more frequently than they'll express their thanks. You also know that much of what you do behind the scenes will never receive a word of praise. Of course, that's not why you do it. You do what you do out of love. The same is true of God. Take some time today to praise your heavenly Father for all the little ways He shows His love.

POWER SOURCE

We are like clay jars in which this treasure is stored.
The real power comes from God and not from us.

2 Corinthians 4:7 cev

. . . .

What happens if your blow-dryer won't blow? First, you check out the power source. Without power, a blow-dryer may look useful, but it's really nothing more than a hunk of plastic and metal. Likewise, it's God's power working through you that allows you to accomplish more than you can on your own. Staying connected with God through prayer, obedience, reading the Bible, and loving others well will keep His power flowing freely into your life—and out into the world.

WORRIES INTO PRAYERS

Don't fret or worry. Instead of worrying, pray.
Let petitions and praises shape your worries into
prayers, letting God know your concerns.

PHILIPPIANS 4:6 MSG

Sometimes it feels like it's a woman's job to worry. If you can't be assured that all your loved ones' physical and emotional needs are being met, fretting about them makes you feel involved—like you're loving them, even if you're powerless to help. But you know someone who does have the power to help. Anytime you feel the weight of worry, whether it's over someone else's problems or your own, let faith relieve you of the burden. Turn your worries into prayers.

JOYFUL ARE THOSE

*Praise the Lord! How joyful are those who fear
the Lord and delight in obeying his commands.
Their children will be successful everywhere; an
entire generation of godly people will be blessed.*

Psalm 112:1–2 nlt

. . . .

When we're fully aware of God's love for us—and for our children—we can
be more than satisfied. We can be joyful! Why? Because He has us covered.
He sees our needs and meets them. He loves us with an everlasting love.
And His blessings aren't just for us; they're for an entire generation of
godly people! Talk about a reason to celebrate!

LOVE COVERS ALL WRONGS

"I tell you, her sins—and they are many—have been forgiven, so she has shown me much love. But a person who is forgiven little shows only little love."

LUKE 7:47 NLT

• •

If you've ever been forgiven for something you considered really grievous, then you know what it means to be grateful! Love covers all wrongs. It also forgives on a grand scale. To extend this kind of forgiveness, you have to genuinely love the other person, both in word and deed. Love big. Forgive big.

GENTLE STRENGTH

Always be prepared to give an answer to everyone
who asks you to give the reason for the hope that you
have. But do this with gentleness and respect.
1 PETER 3:15 NIV

From surgery to intricate cookie decorating, it takes a gentle hand to accomplish a delicate task. But sometimes gentleness is viewed as a sign of weakness. Gentleness is not less powerful or effective than strength. It's strength released in a controlled, appropriate measure. When sharing your faith, gentleness shows you care for others the way God does. Jesus was never pushy. He simply told the truth. Then He allowed others the freedom to choose what to do with it.

"YES!"

We keep praying that God will make you worthy of being his people. We pray for God's power to help you do all the good things you hope to do and your faith makes you want to do.

2 Thessalonians 1:11 cev

Faith gives you the desire—and power—to do things you may have never even dreamed of attempting before. Serving meals to the homeless. Leading a Bible study. Praying for an ailing coworker. Sharing your personal story aloud. Forgiving someone who's betrayed you. The more you grow in your faith, the more God will stretch your idea of who you are—and what you can do. Through God's power, you can confidently say "yes!" to doing anything He asks.

LEAN ON HIM

Consider him who endured such opposition from sinners,
so that you will not grow weary and lose heart.
HEBREWS 12:3 NIV

. . . .

Jesus literally went through hell for you. He suffered the pain of rejection and betrayal. He endured physical agony. He gave His life out of love for you, to bring glory to His Father. When you face what seems unendurable, hold on to Jesus. Cry out to Him for help and hope. Pray throughout the day, picturing Him by your side, holding you up when your own strength fails. Express your love for Him by leaning on Him. He's near to help you persevere.

HEAD-ON

*If you had faith no larger than a mustard seed, you could
tell this mountain to move from here to there.
And it would. Everything would be possible for you.*

MATTHEW 17:20 CEV

The Bible tells us faith is what moves mountains. Not personal ability. Not perseverance. Not even prayer. These can all play a part in facing a challenge that looks as immovable as a mountain. But it's faith in God's ability, not our own, that's the first step toward meeting a challenge head-on—then conquering it. Remind yourself of what's true about God's loving character and incomparable power. Then move toward the challenge instead of away from it. God's in control.

WITH LONG LIFE

"I will reward them with a long life and give them my salvation."
PSALM 91:16 NLT

Have you ever seen the look of contentment in the face of an older believer? Next time you're around folks in their golden years, take time to examine their demeanor. What you will find is contentment. Satisfaction. They've walked with God a long time and know that the Lord won't leave or forsake them. They have seen God's salvation in this lifetime and look forward to heaven, which is right around the bend.

GIVING THANKS

" 'There will be heard once more the sounds of joy and gladness, the voices of bride and bridegroom, and the voices of those who bring thank offerings to the house of the LORD, saying, "Give thanks to the LORD Almighty, for the LORD is good; his love endures forever." For I will restore the fortunes of the land as they were before,' says the LORD."
JEREMIAH 33:10–11 NIV

One of the ways we "give" is to give thanks to the Lord. How easy it is to forget to thank Him for His many blessings. When we see His love for us, when we realize that He's never going to leave us or forsake us, we're motivated to give thanks. And as we lift our voices in praise, others are watching. We're teaching them to offer words of thanks to God as well!

LET GOODNESS FLOW

Whenever we have the opportunity, we should do good to everyone—especially to those in the family of faith.

GALATIANS 6:10 NLT

You can't be a good woman without doing good things. That isn't a rule. It's more of a reminder. Goodness flows naturally from a faith-filled heart. As you grow in your faith, you're changed from the inside out. You become more loving as you draw closer to our loving God. Your once prideful, self-centered heart begins to put others' needs before your own. Say yes to letting goodness flow freely from your life into the lives of others.

A FRESH START

*I have fought the good fight, I have finished
the race, I have kept the faith.*

2 Timothy 4:7 nkjv

Faith is more like a marathon than a leisurely jog through the park. During some legs of the race, you'll be feeling strong and confident. During others, you may find yourself stumbling over questions, losing sight of the right path, or wanting to sit on the sidelines. To keep moving forward, run the race of faith one step at a time. Consider each day a fresh starting line. Moment by moment, with God's help, you will persevere.

GOOD MEALS

He satisfies the longing soul,
and fills the hungry soul with goodness.

PSALM 107:9 NKJV

· ·

When you're preparing a holiday meal, chances are you don't settle for "good enough." You rely on your favorite dishes—recipes that look good, taste good, and are good for you. God feeds your soul similar spiritual fare. Like a good cook who consistently turns out good meals, our good God consistently bestows good gifts. Sometimes they're delectable delights. Other times they're much-needed vegetables. You can trust in God's goodness to serve up exactly what you need.

OPPORTUNITIES

Anyone who meets a testing challenge head-on and manages to stick it out is mighty fortunate. For such persons loyally in love with God, the reward is life and more life.

JAMES 1:12 MSG

People joke about how women sit around eating bonbons all day. You know firsthand nothing is further from the truth. You face challenges each and every day. Instead of viewing challenges as negative, faith helps you see them as opportunities for growth. Building a strong body is difficult and often uncomfortable, and strengthening your faith can be the same way. But the outcome is worth the challenge. A stronger faith results in a more balanced life.

UNDER THE SHADOW

How precious is your unfailing love, O God! All humanity
finds shelter in the shadow of your wings.
PSALM 36:7 NLT

People fail us. They say they're going to do something, and then they don't. They promise to stick with us, and then they leave. We even fail others, making promises we don't keep. But God isn't a failure, and neither is His love. We can trust in His unfailing love. In fact, we can live under its shadow all the days of our lives!

LOVE DEEPLY

Above all, love each other deeply,
because love covers over a multitude of sins.

1 Peter 4:8 niv

It's human nature to withhold forgiveness in order to teach the other person a lesson, but that's not God's way. He doesn't want us to wait too long to forgive. His desire is that we're honest with each other when we're upset. After all, we all sin and fall short. We have to be willing to go the distance and do what it takes to mend fences. How do we accomplish this? Love deeply.

BY GRACE ALONE

God saved you by his grace when you believed.
And you can't take credit for this; it is a gift from God.
EPHESIANS 2:8 NLT

• •

It's humbling to accept a favor from someone, especially when you know it's one you can never repay. But that's what grace is: a gift so big you don't deserve it and can never repay it. All God asks is a tiny, mustard seed–sized grain of faith in return. When you tell God, "I believe," His grace wipes away everything that once came between you and Him. Lies. Anger. Betrayal. Pride. Selfishness. They're history, by God's grace alone.

A PERFECT COMPLEMENT

"I am leaving you with a gift—peace of mind and heart. And the peace I give is a gift the world cannot give. So don't be troubled or afraid."

JOHN 14:27 NLT

When attending a going-away party, it's customary to give a gift to the one who's leaving. Jesus turned this concept on its head, as He so often did with the status quo. At the Last Supper, the day before He died, Jesus gave all of His followers a gift—peace. When you choose to follow Jesus, you receive this gift. You'll find it fits your life perfectly, complementing any and every circumstance.

ULTIMATE MAKEOVER

Don't become so well-adjusted to your culture that you fit into it without even thinking. Instead, fix your attention on God. You'll be changed from the inside out.

ROMANS 12:2 MSG

You're no longer the woman you once were. When you put your faith in God, you experience the ultimate makeover. You're totally forgiven. You're empowered to be able to do whatever God asks. Your old habits lose their grip over you. But continued growth and change is a joint effort between you and God. If there's any area in your life that seems resistant to change, talk to God about it right now—and every morning until change takes place.

UNQUENCHABLE LOVE

*Many waters cannot quench love; rivers cannot sweep
it away. If one were to give all the wealth of one's
house for love, it would be utterly scorned.*
SONG OF SONGS 8:7 NIV

Have you ever been so thirsty that a cup of water didn't satisfy you? If so, then you have some understanding of how love works. The more you have of it, the more you want. And God's love for us is so overpowering that nothing we do can wash it away. Talk about amazing love! Lift up your voice in praise for the love you've been shown.

PERMANENT PEACE

Since we have been made right in God's sight by faith, we have peace with God because of what Jesus Christ our Lord has done for us.

ROMANS 5:1 NLT

. . . .

When world leaders sign a peace treaty, they pledge to keep the terms of an agreement. They aren't agreeing to like it—or each other. When you put your faith in Christ's sacrifice on your behalf, you make peace with God. God pledges to forgive your past grievances and even future mistakes. But the peace between you and God is more than an agreement. It's the rebirth of a relationship. This peace is permanent, based not on legality, but on unconditional love.

UNFAILING LOVE

Even though on the outside it often looks like things are falling apart on us, on the inside, where God is making new life, not a day goes by without his unfolding grace.

2 Corinthians 4:16 MSG

When you first chose to believe in God, His grace wiped away every past detour you'd ever made from the life He designed for you to lead. But His grace doesn't stop there. Every day, it's at work. You may be God's daughter, but you're still growing. There'll be times you'll stumble. Times you'll look to yourself first, instead of to God. God's grace continues to cleanse you and draw you closer to Him, reassuring you of His unfailing love.

"ADIEU!"

"Forget the former things; do not dwell on the past. See, I am doing a new thing! Now it springs up; do you not perceive it?"
ISAIAH 43:18–19 NIV

. . . .

Change is a combination of embracing and letting go. When you become a mom, you welcome new love and bid "adieu" to some former freedoms. When you put your faith in God, you embrace the guidance of God's Spirit and abandon your old, self-centered agenda. When times get tough, it's tempting to seek comfort by looking to the past. But life only moves in one direction. Forward. Only by letting go of yesterday can you welcome today's opportunities with open arms.

LOVE AS YOU SAY YOU LOVE

Many claim to have unfailing love, but a
faithful person who can find?
PROVERBS 20:6 NIV

• •

"I love yous" are a dime a dozen. We hear them on TV, read them in books, and see them in gossip magazines. Everyone is in love, though usually not for long. Though they say the words, many would-be lovers change their minds after a short time. If you're looking for a forever love, look to God. He loves as He says He loves, and He can teach you to do the same!

KEEP WALKING

*Keep your eyes on Jesus, who both began and
finished this race we're in. Study how he did it. . . .
He never lost sight of where he was headed.*

HEBREWS 12:2 MSG

When following a trail, you're really following those who came before you. Physically, they're no longer present. But you can follow what they left behind. Maybe a sign points you in the proper direction. Perhaps you walk a path flattened by previous footsteps. Keep your eyes on Jesus the way you follow a trail. Read what other followers left behind—the Bible. Watch for signs of God's work in the world. Then keep walking, leaving a "faith trail" others can follow.

TESTING. . .

Test yourselves and find out if you really are true to your faith.
If you pass the test, you will discover that Christ is living
in you. But if Christ isn't living in you, you have failed.
2 CORINTHIANS 13:5 CEV

. . . .

As a kid, you took plenty of tests. Your SAT score was determined by how your efforts measured up to a set standard. As a woman of faith, it's time for another test: Measure your character against the woman God desires you to become. This isn't a test God grades. It's simply a tool to help you know where your faith needs to grow. Best of all, this is a group project. Jesus is working both in you and through you.

UNSHAKEN AND UNFAILING

*"Though the mountains be shaken and the hills be removed,
yet my unfailing love for you will not be shaken nor my covenant of
peace be removed," says the LORD, who has compassion on you.*
ISAIAH 54:10 NIV

. . . .

Life doesn't always go the way we hope it does. We face storms. Challenges. We're wounded by people we love, and we feel like curling up in a ball and forgetting about life. God's unfailing love woos us from our place of pain and reminds us that the shaking won't last forever. His covenant of peace lasts forever. We really can be unshaken, as long as we abide in His unfailing love.

A SAVIOR WHO UNDERSTANDS

*While he was still speaking, there came a crowd,
and the man called Judas, one of the twelve,
was leading them. He drew near to Jesus to kiss him.*
LUKE 22:47 ESV

Have you ever been betrayed by someone you thought you could trust? Jesus can relate. Imagine how He must have felt watching one of the disciples He loved turn on Him and sell Him out for thirty pieces of silver. Perhaps you feel as if you've been sold out by a friend or loved one. Follow the example of Jesus, who, even in the face of betrayal, chose to forgive.

THE RIGHT DIRECTION

Each morning let me learn more about your love because I trust you. I come to you in prayer, asking for your guidance.
PSALM 143:8 CEV

If you're navigating a road trip, just owning a map isn't going to get you to your destination. You need to compare where you are on the map with where you want to go, follow road signs, and evaluate your progress. God's Spirit works in much the same way. Each morning ask Him to help you head in the right direction. Then throughout the day, evaluate whether you are where and who you believe God wants you to be.

SURPRISED BY HAPPINESS

You will come to know God even better. His glorious power will make you patient and strong enough to endure anything, and you will be truly happy.

COLOSSIANS 1:10–11 CEV

Faith is a journey. Like any journey, it's a mixed bag of experiences. You can celebrate grand vistas then slog through bogs of mud—all in the same day. Though happiness is often dependent on circumstances, when your journey's guided by faith you can find yourself feeling happy at the most unexpected moments. Perhaps God brings a Bible verse to mind that encourages you. Maybe you see Him at work in a "coincidence." Where will God surprise you with happiness today?

PASS IT ON

Each of you is now a new person. You are becoming more and more like your Creator, and you will understand him better.
Colossians 3:10 cev

• •

Moms pass on lots of things to their children, like the shape of their nose or color of their eyes. They can also pass on things like speech patterns or food preferences. That's because when you spend time together, you pick up the habits of those you're with. In the same way, the more time you spend with God, the more your character begins to resemble His. That's a family likeness worth celebrating.

WITH ALL YOUR HEART

*Jesus said to him, " 'You shall love the L*ORD *your God with all your heart, with all your soul, and with all your mind.'*
This is the first and great commandment. And the second is like it: 'You shall love your neighbor as yourself.' On these two commandments hang all the Law and the Prophets."
MATTHEW 22:37–40 NKJV

Jesus commands us to do two things: Love God and love others. That seems so simple, yet it's so hard! If we truly loved God with all of our hearts—laying down our own wants, wishes, and desires—it would revolutionize our lives! Here's the great part: It's possible to live like this! Love God. Love people. Watch as God transforms your world!

I WILL BOW DOWN

I will bow down toward your holy temple and will praise your
name for your unfailing love and your faithfulness, for you have
so exalted your solemn decree that it surpasses your fame.
PSALM 138:2 NIV

Sometimes we come into God's presence and we feel like shouting for joy.
At other times His love drives us to our knees. Oh, how we're humbled by
what He has done for us. We kneel in His presence and praise His name,
not just for His gifts, but also for His moment-by-moment offering of love.
Our God is worthy to be praised!

MORE TO LOVE

*Make me as happy as you did when you
saved me; make me want to obey!*
PSALM 51:12 CEV

Relationships grow and change. If you're in a marriage relationship, recall that honeymoon phase. Loving each other seemed easy and exciting, pretty much all the time. Then came everyday life. Apathy crept in. The happiness you first felt seemed to fade. The same thing can happen with God. Don't settle for apathy when there's always more to love and discover about God. (And people!) Ask God to help you look at those you love, including Him, with fresh eyes.

SPIRITUAL HEALTH CARE

*The prayer offered in faith will make
the sick person well; the Lord will raise them up.
If they have sinned, they will be forgiven.*

JAMES 5:15 NIV

Prayer is God's spiritual health-care plan. Modern medicine can do wonderful things to help a sick person get well. But God knows your body better than anyone. He designed it. He can heal it. Not every prayer for healing is answered in the way and time frame we hope for. Sometimes emotional or spiritual healing takes place, while physical healing does not. God can raise us up in different ways. So call on Him. You never need an appointment.

LIMITLESS

LORD, you know the hopes of the helpless.
Surely you will hear their cries and comfort them.
PSALM 10:17 NLT

· ·

There's only so much one woman can do. There are limits to your strength, your time, and your capacity to love others well. When you reach the limit of your own abilities, a feeling of helplessness can set in. But being helpless isn't synonymous with being hopeless. God is near. He hears every prayer, every longing, and every sigh. His power, love, and time are limitless. Cry out in faith when you need the comfort of your Father's love.

ENCOURAGE ONE ANOTHER

[Let us] not [give] up meeting together, as some are in
the habit of doing, but [let us encourage] one another—
and all the more as you see the Day approaching.
HEBREWS 10:25 NIV

. . . .

Don't you love the encouragement you receive from your brothers and
sisters in Christ? They pour out God's love on you and vice versa. Together
the body of Christ is a force to be reckoned with! And in these end times,
we need each other more than ever! With all of your heart, love your
fellow believers.

SAFE IN HIS ARMS

My health may fail, and my spirit may grow weak,
but God remains the strength of my heart; he is mine forever.
PSALM 73:26 NLT

Our bodies are miraculous works of art. But they don't last forever. When you're ill or in pain, God is near. As any parent who's ever loved a child knows, He aches with you, as well as for you. When the hope of healing seems distant, if you've run out of words to pray, picture yourself safe in His arms. Wait quietly, expectantly. Listen for His words of comfort. Rest in His promised peace. Hold on to Him for strength.

CHANGED HEARTS

For whatever things were written before were written
for our learning, that we through the patience and
comfort of the Scriptures might have hope.

ROMANS 15:4 NKJV

Reading how women like us have faced difficult circumstances yet found peace, power, and purpose through faith can be a source of comfort. Whether the account is about Lazarus' sisters Mary and Martha, the woman caught in adultery, or the Samaritan at the well, these women all found comfort in Christ's words. In turn, we can be comforted by their experience. Just as Christ changed their hearts and lives, His words and His love can do the same for us today.

THE UNEXPECTED

Jesus replied, "Why do you say 'if you can'?
Anything is possible for someone who has faith!"
MARK 9:23 CEV

What can we expect from God? The unexpected. Many people who came to Jesus asked to be healed. But how Jesus healed them was never the same. He put mud in a blind man's eyes. A bleeding woman merely touched His robe. Sometimes, Jesus spoke—and healing happened. Coming to God in faith means you can expect that He will act. He promises He'll respond to your prayers. How? Anticipate the unexpected.

ANYTIME, ANYWHERE

Get up and pray for help all through the night. Pour out your feelings to the Lord, as you would pour water out of a jug.
LAMENTATIONS 2:19 CEV

There's probably no more common prayer than the word *help*. Even those who aren't aware they're calling out to the living God cry out for help in times of despair, fear, or pain. But you know God is near. You know He hears. In faith, you believe He will help. Regardless of your circumstance—big or small—don't wait until you come to the end of your rope to pray. Call out to Him anytime, anywhere.

INVITE GOD

God is our refuge and strength, a very present help in trouble.
PSALM 46:1 NKJV

Real life doesn't resemble what's seen on TV. Problems aren't resolved in an hour's time. There may be seasons where you need God's help just to make it through today and tomorrow and the day after that. During times like these, God's presence can be a place of rest and refuge. Go for a walk. Draw a bubble bath. Find a quiet spot to just sit. Then invite God to join you. Allow Him to refresh you with His love.

LIFE PRESERVER

Cling to your faith in Christ.
1 Timothy 1:19 NLT

. . . .

If you were shipwrecked, you'd cling to your life preserver in hope of rescue. Faith is your life preserver in this world. It keeps your head above water in life and carries you safely into God's arms after death. But it takes commitment to keep holding on tightly. Emotions rise and fall. Circumstances ebb and flow. But God is committed to you. His love and faithfulness never fail. By holding tightly to your faith, you can weather any storm.

MORE REASONS TO HOPE

*Let us hold unswervingly to the hope we profess,
for he who promised is faithful.*
HEBREWS 10:23 NIV

What do you hope for? Really hope for? Perhaps it's security, significance, or a relationship that will never let you down. Hopes like these are fulfilled solely through faith. Read God's track record in the Bible. He keeps His promises in every area time and again. It's true that it takes faith to place your hope in someone you can't see. But you're building your own track record with God. Day by day, you'll discover more reasons to hope in Him.

....

....

....

....

....

....

....

....

....

....

JOINED TOGETHER

Instead, speaking the truth in love, we will grow to become in every respect the mature body of him who is the head, that is, Christ. From him the whole body, joined and held together by every supporting ligament, grows and builds itself up in love, as each part does its work.

EPHESIANS 4:15–16 NIV

. . . .

Love graces us through our mistakes and joins us together as one body, the bride of Christ. We learn how to love by reading the Bible and spending time with God, who gave us the ultimate example of how to love when He sent His Son to die in our place. All He asks in return is that we give our hearts to Him. Go forth and love, dear friends!

GIVE THANKS TO THE LORD

*After consulting the people, Jehoshaphat appointed men to
sing to the LORD and to praise him for the splendor of his
holiness as they went out at the head of the army, saying:
"Give thanks to the LORD, for his love endures forever."*

2 CHRONICLES 20:21 NIV

Don't you love early mornings? They're filled with promise. New day. New dawn. New chance to experience God's awesome love. He is pleased when we make a choice to give thanks early in the day. His enduring love never sleeps, so it meets us fresh every morning. Praise Him for that unfailing love, even before your eyes are fully open!

HOPE OF HEAVEN

What you hope for is kept safe for you in heaven.
You first heard about this hope when you believed
the true message, which is the good news.

COLOSSIANS 1:5 CEV

Faith gives us many reasons for hope. A home in heaven is just one of them. But what exactly are you hoping for? The Bible tells us we'll receive a new body, one that never grows ill or old. Tears will be a thing of the past. We'll be in the company of angels, other believers, and God Himself. Scripture tells us words cannot fully describe what we'll find there. That's a hope worth holding on to.

FOLLOW THROUGH

*By faith the walls of Jericho fell, after the army
had marched around them for seven days.*
HEBREWS 11:30 NIV

In the Bible, God asks people to do some seemingly strange things. Build an ark. Defeat Jericho by walking around its walls. Battle a giant with a slingshot. But when people are committed to doing what God asks, amazing things happen. What's God asking you to do? Love someone who seems unlovable? Break a bad habit? Forgive? Commit yourself to follow through and do what God asks. Through faith, you'll witness firsthand how the unbelievable can happen.

ABOUNDING. . .MORE AND MORE!

And it is my prayer that your love may abound more and more, with knowledge and all discernment, so that you may approve what is excellent, and so be pure and blameless for the day of Christ, filled with the fruit of righteousness that comes through Jesus Christ, to the glory and praise of God.
PHILIPPIANS 1:9–11 ESV

Have you ever watched a snowball roll down a hill? As it picks up speed, it begins to grow! Before long, it's huge and powerful! That's how love is. The more love you share, the more you get. The longer we love, the more we have the capacity to love. If you're hoping to receive more, try giving it away. Then get ready for the snowball effect!

WHO DO YOU SEE?

*Do not think of yourself more highly than you ought,
but rather think of yourself with sober judgment, in accordance
with the faith God has distributed to each of you.*
ROMANS 12:3 NIV

A humble woman sees herself through God's eyes. She recognizes the unique strengths God has built into her character. She sees herself as a creative collage of personality traits, talents, and abilities. But she's also well aware of her weaknesses. She knows that without God, even her strengths would not be enough to catapult her into becoming the woman she wants to be. Look at yourself through God's eyes today. What do you see?

IN STYLE

Therefore, as God's chosen people, holy and dearly loved, clothe yourselves with compassion, kindness, humility, gentleness and patience.

Colossians 3:12 niv

• •

Before you leave the house, chances are you make sure you're appropriately dressed. You don't head out to a business meeting in your PJs, to the grocery store in your swimsuit, or off for a jog in heels. Faith offers you a different kind of wardrobe, one that's appropriate for every occasion. By clothing yourself in compassion, you reflect God's very own style—a style that prepares you for anything.

I HAVE COME THAT YOU MIGHT HAVE LIFE

A thief comes only to rob, kill, and destroy. I came so everyone would have life, and have it fully.
JOHN 10:10 CEV

. . . .

Don't you just love life? It's filled with unexpected and undeserved joys. Sure, not every day is a piece of cake, but we're alive and well today and have hope for tomorrow. God's love for us is so deep that He came to earth so that we could have life. . .and not just any life. He wants us to have abundant life. That's a "more than I could ask or think" life.

THE ULTIMATE GARDENER

In simple humility, let our gardener, God, landscape you
with the Word, making a salvation-garden of your life.
JAMES 1:21 MSG

Some women have a bona fide green thumb. They take a seemingly dead stick and nurture it into a verdant piece of paradise. Consider how ridiculous it would be for that once sickly stick to brag to foliage friends about the great turnaround it had accomplished on its own. Obviously, all credit goes to the gardener. God is the ultimate gardener. His focus is tending His children. Humbly allow Him to have His way in helping your faith grow.

FULLY LIVE

I will be careful to live a blameless life—when will you come to help me? I will lead a life of integrity in my own home.

PSALM 101:2 NLT

One of the hardest places to consistently live out what you believe is in your own home. That's because those who know you best have seen you at your worst. Living a life of integrity 24/7 takes more than self-control. It takes a change of heart. Only God can transform a selfish, wayward ego into a woman worth emulating. Place your faith in God's power, lay aside your pride, and then fully live what you say you believe.

DEEPER THAN A MOTHER'S LOVE

*"Can a mother forget the baby at her breast and
have no compassion on the child she has borne?
Though she may forget, I will not forget you!"*
ISAIAH 49:15 NIV

. . . .

A mother's love could be considered the epitome of compassion. A mother selflessly carries a child within her own body for nine months then nourishes the newborn with her own milk. She comforts, weans, cleans, and cuddles. And if the situation arose, most mothers would sacrifice their own lives to save the children they love. Yet God's compassion runs even deeper than a mother's love. His loving care is passionate, powerful, and permanent for those who put their faith in Him.

LOOKING AT THE HEART

"The LORD does not look at the things people look at. People look at the outward appearance, but the LORD looks at the heart."
1 SAMUEL 16:7 NIV

· ·

We tend to judge people by outward appearance, and sometimes the way we treat them is affected as well. Thankfully, God loves us despite our spots and wrinkles! And He calls us to love others in spite of any physical flaws. If you want to show the love of God to friends or coworkers, don't judge them by what they wear, their hairstyles, or their choice of makeup (or lack thereof). Just love them. Period.

A GLIMPSE OF GOD

In the morning, Lord, you hear my voice; in the morning
I lay my requests before you and wait expectantly.

PSALM 5:3 NIV

· ·

If you're expecting an important package, you're often on the lookout for the mail carrier. You peek out the window. Listen for footsteps. Check the mailbox. When you pray, are you on the lookout for God's answers? Not every answer will be delivered when, where, and how you expect. So keep your eyes open and your heart expectant. Don't miss out on the joy of catching a glimpse of God at work.

GOD'S WAY

In everything set them an example by doing what is good. In your teaching show integrity, seriousness and soundness of speech.

TITUS 2:7–8 NIV

• •

It's said that character is who you are in the dark. If integrity is part of that character, you'll do the right thing whether someone's watching or not. It takes faith to remain morally upright, honest, and true to your word in a culture where it's considered acceptable to do the exact opposite in the name of getting ahead. But God's way is ultimately the wisest, most beneficial way. Through your integrity, God may teach others lessons they'll never forget.

....

....

....

....

....

....

....

....

....

....

RESERVE OF JOY

*Though you have not seen him, you love him; and even
though you do not see him now, you believe in him and
are filled with an inexpressible and glorious joy.*

1 Peter 1:8 niv

In the Declaration of Independence, American citizens are guaranteed the right to the "pursuit of happiness." That's probably because happiness is something that must constantly be pursued. Even if you catch it, you can't hold on to it. Joy, on the other hand, is a gift of dependence. The more you depend on God, the deeper your well of joy. Ask God to show you how to draw on that reserve of joy in any and every circumstance.

UNLIKELY WAYS

*When troubles of any kind come your way, consider it an
opportunity for great joy. For you know that when your
faith is tested, your endurance has a chance to grow.*

JAMES 1:2–3 NLT

. . . .

"Trouble" and "joy" may seem an unlikely pair, something akin to sardines
and chocolate syrup. But God seems to prefer the unlikely. He chose
a speech-impaired Moses as His spokesman, and simple fishermen as
missionaries. These choices brought challenges. But when faith is pushed
to its limits, God works in wonderfully unlikely ways. Regard troubles as
opportunities instead of obstacles. As you rely on God, His glory will shine
through you—and unexpected joy will be your reward.

GOD-CONFIDENCE

Forget about self-confidence; it's useless.
Cultivate God-confidence.
1 Corinthians 10:12 MSG

You're a beautiful, gifted woman. God created you that way. You have countless reasons to be confident in what you do, who you are, and where you're headed—but those reasons don't rest on your talents, intelligence, accomplishments, net worth, or good looks. They rest solely on God and His faithfulness. Living a life of faith means trading self-confidence for God-confidence. It means holding your head high because you know you're loved and that God's Spirit is working through you.

FROM EVERLASTING TO EVERLASTING

But from everlasting to everlasting the LORD's love is with those who fear him, and his righteousness with their children's children.
PSALM 103:17 NIV

Isn't it interesting to think that God has existed forever? Before He created the heavens and the earth, He was. And He will be here in the "forever" yet to come as well. Even more amazing, God has been in love with His people forever. He loved humankind in the garden, and He will love us long after we're all in heaven with Him. His love truly reaches from everlasting to everlasting.

A LOVING PROCLAMATION

*"Therefore, my friends, I want you to know that through
Jesus the forgiveness of sins is proclaimed to you."*
ACTS 13:38 NIV

Through Jesus, God offers forgiveness of sins. Think about that for a minute. He has indebted Himself to humankind through Jesus' work on the cross. He paid the debt for our sin! In doing so, God has made a covenant with us: "Love My Son. Accept His free gift of salvation. In exchange, I will offer you forgiveness of sins and eternal life." Oh, what a gift! What a debt of love He paid!

BENEVOLENT BALANCE

*And what does the L<small>ORD</small> require of you? To act justly and
to love mercy and to walk humbly with your God.*
M<small>ICAH</small> 6:8 <small>NIV</small>

· ·

God is both merciful and just. His justice demands that restitution be
made for the wrongs we've done. His mercy allows those wrongs to be
paid for in full when we put our faith in Jesus' death and resurrection.
One way of thanking God for this benevolent balance is by treating others
fairly, mercifully, and with humility. When we do this, we love in a way
that reflects our heavenly Father's own character.

AWED

The Fear-of-God builds up confidence,
and makes a world safe for your children.

PROVERBS 14:26 MSG

· ·

When the Bible talks about the "fear of God," it's more about awe than
alarm. Through faith, we catch a glimpse of how powerful God really is and
how small we are in comparison. Yet the depth of God's love for us rivals
the enormity of His might. Regardless of the troubles that may surround
you or what you see on the evening news, you can be confident that God
remains in charge, in control, and deeply in love.

DRAWN WITH LOVING-KINDNESS

"I have loved you with an everlasting love;
I have drawn you with unfailing kindness."

JEREMIAH 31:3 NIV

· ·

"Infinity" is a difficult concept to grasp. When we say *forever*, we're keenly aware that the forever life goes far beyond what we experience here on earth. When we ask Jesus to come into our hearts and He becomes Lord of our lives, we step into a "forever" existence with Him. And His love lasts forever too. It's not just meant for the here and now, but for all eternity. Praise God for His everlasting love!

SING FOR JOY

But let all who take refuge in you be glad; let them ever sing for joy. Spread your protection over them, that those who love your name may rejoice in you.

PSALM 5:11 NIV

. . . .

There are so many things to rejoice over when you're in love with the Creator of heaven and earth. And rejoicing changes your perspective on everything! Remember that little song you may have sung as a child: "I've got the joy, joy, joy, joy down in my heart!" It's true. Love gives birth to joy. And when that joy spills over, watch out! It's contagious!

ALWAYS RIGHT AND JUST

*Be ready! Let the truth be like a belt around your waist,
and let God's justice protect you like armor.*

Ephesians 6:14 cev

· ·

A Roman soldier's belt was more than a fashion accessory. It held all of his offensive weapons. A soldier's defensive gear included a helmet, breastplate, and shield—his armor. As a woman of faith, God is your armor. When you're under attack, God not only offers you protection; He promises you justice. Secure your life with God's truth. Then rest in the fact that He's working behind the scenes, always doing what is right and just.

BEYOND YOUR COMFORT ZONE

God wants us to have faith in his Son Jesus Christ and to love each other. This is also what Jesus taught us to do.

1 JOHN 3:23 CEV

People matter to God. All kinds of people. From celebrities to "nobodies," pompous people to selfless servants, atheists to those martyred for their faith. If people matter to God, they should also matter to you. It's easy to invest yourself only in relationships that feel comfortable and personally beneficial. But faith sees beyond social circles and stereotypes. Ask God to help you reach beyond your relational comfort zone. You may be surprised by the gift of a friend for life.

FLOURISHING IN GOD'S LOVE

But I am like an olive tree flourishing in the house of God;
I trust in God's unfailing love for ever and ever.
PSALM 52:8 NIV

· ·

When we trust in God's unfailing, everlasting love, we flourish like trees planted by streams of living water. We continue to grow and thrive. As you ponder this forever love that God offers through His Son, trust that He will walk you through the rest of your days stronger than you've ever been. You can flourish in God's everlasting love!

QUIET COMPASSION

You've had a taste of God. Now, like infants at
the breast, drink deep of God's pure kindness.
Then you'll grow up mature and whole in God.

1 Peter 2:2–3 msg

Kindness is the quiet compassion that flows from a loving heart. It doesn't announce its actions with shouts of "Look at me! Look what I did!" It whispers ever so gently, "Look at you. You're so worthy of love. Caring for you is my pleasure, my delight." Being the focus of an almighty King's kindness can be incredibly humbling, as well as encouraging. Let both humility and joy foster gratitude—and growth—in you.

WORDS AND ACTIONS

Everything depends on having faith in God, so that God's promise is assured by his gift of undeserved grace.

ROMANS 4:16 CEV

. . . .

A wise mother schools her children in the ways of kindness not only with her words but through her actions. God works the same way. Through the words of the Bible, God encourages His children to treat each other with respect, generosity, and consideration. But it's God's personal kindnesses to you that encourage your faith. Today, consider the many ways God has been kind to you just this week. How will you respond?

PATH TO CONTENTMENT

*"You're blessed when you're content with just who you are—
no more, no less. That's the moment you find yourselves
proud owners of everything that can't be bought."*
MATTHEW 5:5 MSG

Being content with what you have is one thing. Being content with who you are is quite another. This kind of contentment isn't complacency. It doesn't negate the importance of striving for excellence or encouraging growth and change. It means being at peace with the way God designed you and the life He's given you. This kind of contentment is only available in daily doses. Through faith, seek God and His path to contentment each and every morning.

KNOWING GOD

Whoever does not love does not know God, because God is love.
1 John 4:8 niv

Love isn't always easy, is it? Sometimes it's tough to extend love, particularly when our feelings are hurt or we're wounded in some way. The Bible is clear that God is love. He epitomizes it, in fact. And if we withhold our love from others, even if we feel justified, we break God's heart. If we claim to know Him, we have no choice but to love.

PRIVILEGE

If God has given you leadership ability,
take the responsibility seriously.

ROMANS 12:8 NLT

- -

It's a myth that lemmings will follow each other off a cliff. The same can't be said for people. Some people do unthinkable things as the result of following a leader who isn't worthy of admiration or imitation. If God places you in a position of leadership, whether at home, at work, at church, or in the community, recognize it for the privilege it is. Ask God to help you love those you lead, guiding them with humility and wisdom.

A GODLY LEADER

*Good leadership is a channel of water controlled by
GOD; he directs it to whatever ends he chooses.*
PROVERBS 21:1 MSG

· ·

A good leader is a godly leader. She recognizes her strengths and uses them
in a way that honors God and others. Most importantly, she recognizes
her greatest asset is prayer. If you ask God for wisdom, He promises He'll
give it to you. Whether you're leading executives in the boardroom or
preschoolers through a lesson in sharing, ask God for the right words,
right timing, and right attitude so you can wisely lead others in the right
direction.

PRAY DAILY

Start with God—the first step in learning is bowing down to God; only fools thumb their noses at such wisdom and learning.

PROVERBS 1:7 MSG

. . . .

Before you could read, letters were meaningless squiggles on the page. But with practice and a parent's or teacher's help, one day everything clicked. Squiggles transformed into words—and words into stories. God is like those letters. However, you can't master the art of living by faith simply by studying about God. You need to humbly admit your wrongs. Accept God's forgiveness. Pray daily for growth and guidance. Then you'll learn who God really is and understand your part in His story.

NOTHING TO FEAR

The blood of Jesus gives us courage to enter the most holy place by a new way that leads to life! And this way takes us through the curtain that is Christ himself.
HEBREWS 10:19–20 CEV

Imagine standing before a holy, almighty, and perfect God and being judged for how you've lived your life. Every mistake, poor choice, and moment of rebellion would be exposed. Sounds downright terrifying, doesn't it? But through our faith in Jesus, we have nothing to fear. We stand faultless and forgiven. Through Christ, we can gather the courage to look at ourselves as we really are, faults and all, without shame. Being wholly loved gives us the courage to fully live.

GLORY FOREVER AND EVER

*To him who loves us and has freed us from our sins by his blood,
and has made us to be a kingdom and priests to serve his God and
Father—to him be glory and power for ever and ever! Amen.*

REVELATION 1:5–6 NIV

Oh, how the love of God propels us to praise! His everlasting love has saved us, freed us, and made us His heirs, His children, His own. There's no other place we can go to receive such unconditional love. May we continue to worship Him from now until eternity, offering praise and glory for this spectacular love!

ONE WORTH FOLLOWING

Follow the example of the correct teaching I gave you,
and let the faith and love of Christ Jesus be your model.
2 TIMOTHY 1:13 CEV

• •

The Bible's a pretty lengthy book. It looks like there's a lot to learn. But Jesus said that if we love God and others, we've fulfilled everything written there. How do we do that? Look to Jesus' own life as recorded in the Gospels. Jesus never treats people like an interruption or inconvenience. He listens, comforts, and cares. He spends time with His Father in prayer, regardless of His busy schedule. Jesus' example is one worth following.

NO COMPARISON NECESSARY

We will not compare ourselves with each other as if one of us were better and another worse. We have far more interesting things to do with our lives. Each of us is an original.

GALATIANS 5:26 MSG

When God created each of us, He wove together a wonderful woman unlike any other. But at times it's tempting to gauge how well we're doing by using other women as a measuring stick. Faith offers a different standard. The Bible encourages us to use our abilities in ways that honor God. Some abilities may take center stage, while others work quietly in the background. Just do what you can with what you have in ways that make God smile. No comparison necessary.

EMPOWERED BY PRAYER

*Everything in the Scriptures is God's Word. All of
it is useful for teaching and helping people and for
correcting them and showing them how to live.*
2 Timothy 3:16 cev

Your brain is an amazing, God-given gift. It enables you to master new skills, solve complex problems, and mature in your understanding of life. In short, it enables you to learn. By reading the Bible, you learn how to grow in your faith. As you read, ask yourself, "What does this teach me about loving God and/or others?" Then apply what you learn to your daily life. Your brain, empowered by prayer, will teach you how.

WHATEVER NEEDS DONE

*When I asked for your help, you answered
my prayer and gave me courage.*
PSALM 138:3 CEV

. . . .

Why do you need courage today? To apologize? To forgive? To break an old habit? To discipline a child? To love in the face of rejection? Courage isn't just for times when you're facing grievous danger. Any time you face difficult, unpredictable situations, it takes courage to move forward. When you're tempted to turn away from your problems, let faith help you turn toward God. With Him, you'll find the courage you need to do whatever needs to be done.

FROM GOD'S PERSPECTIVE

*Has not God chosen those who are poor in the eyes
of the world to be rich in faith and to inherit the
kingdom he promised those who love him?*

JAMES 2:5 NIV

Being rich in faith is the secret to leading an abundant life. That's because faith allows us to see life from God's perspective. We begin to appreciate how much we have, instead of focusing on what we think we lack. We understand that what's of eternal worth is more valuable than our net worth. We feel rich, regardless of how much, or how little, we own. True abundance flows from the inside out, from God's hand straight to our hearts.

POWERFUL LESSONS

*Teach believers with your life: by word, by
demeanor, by love, by faith, by integrity.*
1 Timothy 4:12 msg

As a little girl, perhaps you played school before you ever attended class.
If you had the coveted role of teacher, you got to tell your friends what
to do. As an adult, you're still playing the role of teacher, whether you're
aware of it or not. When what you believe changes the way you live and
love, others notice. Who knows? The most powerful lessons you ever
teach may be those where you never say a word.

FOLLOW HARD AFTER GOD

Take me away with you—let us hurry!
Let the king bring me into his chambers.
SONG OF SONGS 1:4 NIV

Have you ever heard the expression "follow hard after God"? To follow Him with passion means that you can't live without Him. This kind of passionate love between God and His people has been going on since the beginning of time. He longs for you to run into His arms so that His love can bring healing in your life. Hurry into His chambers today! There He awaits with arms extended.

RIGHT HERE, RIGHT NOW

Better is one day in your courts than a thousand elsewhere.
PSALM 84:10 NIV

. . . .

It's fun daydreaming about places you'd like to visit, goals you'd like to accomplish, or the woman you hope to mature into—someday. But God's only given you one life. Chances are you'll have more dreams than you'll have days. Instead of living for "someday," God challenges you to put your heart into today. Whether you're sunning on vacation or scrubbing the kitchen floor, the God of the universe is right there with you. That's something worth celebrating!

INTO HIS ARMS

*"Love the LORD your God, walk in all his ways,
obey his commands, hold firmly to him, and serve
him with all your heart and all your soul."*

JOSHUA 22:5 NLT

Every walk you take is a series of steps that moves you forward. Each day you live is like a single step, moving you closer to—or farther away from—God. That's why it's good to get your bearings each morning. Through reading the Bible and spending time with God in prayer, you'll know which direction to take as you continue your walk of faith. Day by day, God will guide you straight into His arms.

EXCEEDED EXPECTATIONS

"I have come that they may have life, and that
they may have it more abundantly."
JOHN 10:10 NKJV

In Jesus' day, the people of Israel were looking for the Messiah promised in scripture. They believed this Savior would restore Israel to its former power and prosperity. Jesus didn't meet their expectations. He exceeded them. Jesus offered them an abundance of riches that couldn't be stolen or lose value, true treasures like joy, peace, forgiveness, and eternal life. Jesus offers these same treasures to you. All you need to do is place your faith in Him.

BEHIND THE SCENES

We make our own decisions, but the LORD
alone determines what happens.
PROVERBS 16:33 CEV

• •

From the man you choose to marry to how you style your hair, decisions are part of your daily life. But that doesn't mean you're totally in control. Much of life is out of your hands and solely in God's. That's where faith provides a place of peace. Rest in the knowledge that God is working behind the scenes to bring about good in your life. The best decision you'll ever make is to trust in His love for you.

FREE WILL

*I pray that your love will keep on growing and you will fully
know and understand how to make the right choices.*
Philippians 1:9–10 cev

Free will is a wonderful gift. It allows you to have a say in the story line of
your life. But there are consequences tied to every decision you make, big
or small. That's why making wise decisions is so important. The more you
allow your faith to influence the decisions you make, the closer you'll be
to living the life God desires for you. Invite God into your decision process.
Let your "yes" or "no" be preceded by "amen."

FEED MY LAMBS

*When they had finished eating, Jesus said to Simon
Peter, "Simon son of John, do you love me more
than these?" "Yes, Lord," he said, "you know that
I love you." Jesus said, "Feed my lambs."*

JOHN 21:15 NIV

• •

What an earthshaking question Jesus asked Peter, His beloved disciple.
"Peter, do you love me more than these?" How would you answer that
question? Surely you would cry out, as Peter did, "Yes, Lord! You know
I do!" But Jesus' response to His followers will always be the same: "If
you love me, care for my children." We're forever indebted to love others
in the body of Christ.

ROOT OF DESIRE

"Wherever your treasure is, there the
desires of your heart will also be."
MATTHEW 6:21 NLT

• •

What does your heart long for? If you look at the root of every deep desire, you'll find something only God can fill. Love, security, comfort, significance, joy. . .trying to satisfy these desires apart from God can only yield limited success. God is the only one whose love for you will never waver. You're His treasure, and His desire is to spend eternity with you. As your faith grows, so will your desire to treasure Him in return.

INCREDIBLE POTENTIAL

As obedient children, let yourselves be pulled into a way of life shaped by God's life, a life energetic and blazing with holiness.

1 PETER 1:15 MSG

Your life has incredible potential. It's filled with opportunities to love, laugh, learn, and make a positive difference in this world. Faith turns every opportunity into an invitation: Will you choose to live this moment in a way that honors God? What you do with your life matters. But ultimately, who you become is more important than what you accomplish. As your faith grows, your heart more resembles God's own. That's when you recognize where your true potential lies.

PART OF LIFE

Jesus said to her, "I am the resurrection and the life.
He who believes in Me, though he may die, he shall live."
JOHN 11:25 NKJV

. . . .

Death is a part of life, at least on this earth. But because of Jesus, death is not something to be feared. It's a door leading from this life into the next. Faith is the key that opens that door. Whenever this life leaves you questioning, hurting, or longing for heaven, picture yourself grasping that key. The more tightly you hold on to your faith, the more peace, hope, and joy you'll experience on this side of that door.

COMPLETELY!

*The Spirit makes us sure God will accept us
because of our faith in Christ.*
GALATIANS 5:5 CEV

. . . .

God accepts you completely. You don't need to clean up your language, change your lifestyle, or step inside of a church. Once you put your faith in Jesus, things between you and God are made right. Period. But acceptance is only the first step in this relationship. As God's Spirit continues working in your heart, He gives you the desire and strength you need to mature into who you were created to be—an amazing woman whose character reflects God's.

THE MOST EXCELLENT WAY

*And yet I will show you the most excellent way. If I speak
in the tongues of men or of angels, but do not have love,
I am only a resounding gong or a clanging cymbal.*
1 CORINTHIANS 12:31–13:1 NIV

. . . .

If you've ever navigated a rocky path in the dark without a flashlight, you
have some small taste of what it would be like to go through life without
love. You could probably make it from point A to point B, but what a rough
trip! In the scripture above, God shows us the most excellent way to make
the journey. Let love light the way!

MAKE THE FIRST MOVE

God sets the lonely in families.
PSALM 68:6 NIV

. . . .

In the beginning of the Bible, God says it isn't good for people to be alone. Then He introduces Adam to Eve. The rest is history. Family is God's idea—and it's a good one. Whether it's your own family, your brothers and sisters in faith, or a time-tested circle of familial friends, don't wait for others to reach out to you when you're feeling lonely. Make the first move. True love both gives and receives.

MOTIVATION

You are no longer ruled by your desires,
but by God's Spirit, who lives in you.
Romans 8:9 cev

In preparing to play a role, an actress asks herself, "What's my character's motivation?" That's because what motivates us, moves us. If a character's desire is to be admired, rich, beautiful, or loved, that will influence her decisions and actions. As you allow God to work in and through you, your desires begin to fall in line with His own. There's no longer any need to act. You're free to be exactly who God created you to be.

LOVING ACCEPTANCE

Accept other believers who are weak in faith, and don't argue with them about what they think is right or wrong.

ROMANS 14:1 NLT

Talking about faith can get tricky at times. What you believe, and how faith plays a part in your everyday life, may differ from those around you—even from those who attend the same church. Faith is important. But so is love and acceptance. God wholeheartedly accepts each and every one of His children and asks that we do the same. Listen in love. Learning to accept others the way Jesus did is more important than always seeing eye to eye.

NEVER ALONE

Jesus often withdrew to lonely places and prayed.
LUKE 5:16 NIV

Loneliness can make you feel like you're on a desert island surrounded by a sea of people—yet no one notices you're there. But there is someone who notices. Someone who'll never leave you. Someone who won't forget you or ignore you, no matter what you've done. You may be lonely, but you're never alone. Find a place of solace in the silence through prayer. Loneliness may be the perfect lifeline to draw you closer to God, the one whose love will never fail.

FAITH ON THE MOVE

All the believers devoted themselves to the apostles'
teaching, and to fellowship, and to sharing in meals
(including the Lord's Supper), and to prayer.
ACTS 2:42 NLT

The time we set aside to read the Bible and pray each day is often called "daily devotions." Have you ever considered why? Think about what it means to be devoted to your husband, your kids, or your job. Devotion is the commitment of yourself to something or someone you love. The same is true with spiritual devotion. Your spiritual faith is a commitment to love God. And since the word *love* is a verb, an action word, your devotion to God is faith on the move. Where will faith move you today?

CELEBRATE!

*We remember before our God and Father your work
produced by faith, your labor prompted by love, and your
endurance inspired by hope in our Lord Jesus Christ.*
1 Thessalonians 1:3 niv

When you work hard toward completing a goal, accomplishing what you've set out to do is something worth celebrating. When your accomplishment is fueled by faith, you can be certain you'll never celebrate alone. God sees the time, energy, and heart you put into your work. Better yet, He adds His own power to your efforts. This means that with God, you can accomplish things you could never do solely on your own. That's something truly worth celebrating—with God!

A HAPPY ENDING

Because you kept on believing, you'll get what you're looking forward to: total salvation.
1 PETER 1:9 MSG

· ·

Your salvation comes through faith in Christ. The result of that salvation is eternal life. Though you're not home in heaven yet, that doesn't mean its existence isn't relevant to you right now. Holding on to your hope of heaven gives you an eternal perspective. It frees you from the fear of death, inspires you to tell others about God's everlasting love, and reminds you that no matter what you face in this life, you're guaranteed a happy ending.

SET IN STONE

*We humans keep brainstorming options
and plans, but God's purpose prevails.*
PROVERBS 19:21 MSG

. . . .

When people mention "the best-laid plans," they're usually bemoaning how the unexpected derailed what once seemed like a sure thing. God's the Master of the unexpected. That doesn't mean planning is a bad thing. It helps us use time, money, and resources in a more efficient way. But the only plans that are set in stone are God's own. Make sure your plans are in line with God's purposes. That's the wisest thing you can do to assure success.

LET LOVE SHINE

What if I had faith that moved mountains?
I would be nothing, unless I loved others.
1 Corinthians 13:2 cev

. . . .

What mountain are you facing today? Perhaps it's the reconciliation of a relationship. Or maybe it's just that pile of laundry you've neglected. Whatever it is, it would be nice to simply "pray it away." But faith isn't a gift God gives to make life easier. Faith is God's classroom in which we learn how to become more loving—more like God Himself. Ask God to let love shine through in everything you do. Even sorting kids' socks.

AWARE OF THE DETAILS

*By faith we understand that the universe was
formed at God's command, so that what is seen
was not made out of what was visible.*

HEBREWS 11:3 NIV

It takes faith and science to appreciate the wonders of nature. Science describes the improbability of generations of butterflies migrating thousands of miles to specific destinations they've never experienced firsthand or the impossibly delicate balance of our orbiting solar system. Faith assures us God not only understands miracles like these but set them in motion. Surely, a God who cares for the tiniest detail of nature is aware—and at work—in every detail of your life.

DEVOTED TO OTHERS

Women who claim to be devoted to God should make themselves attractive by the good things they do.

1 TIMOTHY 2:10 NLT

Our devotion to God leads us to be more devoted to others. That's because God's Spirit is at work in us, encouraging us to do what's right. When we keep our promises, weigh our words, and offer a helping hand with no expectation of reward, we are loving God by loving others. Our faith-filled devotion to God brings out the best in us, while at the same time it blesses those around us.

OVERFLOWING WITH HOPE

We live by faith, not by sight.
2 Corinthians 5:7 niv

Faith changes how we see the world. From all appearances, your circumstances may seem daunting. Your opportunities limited. Your future set in stone. But when you place your faith in God instead of what you see, your heart can't help but overflow with hope. God's power is at work behind the scenes. He's working in both you and your circumstances. He promises to bring something good out of every situation, no matter how things may look on the outside.

TRANSFORMED DOUBTS

*Immediately the father of the child cried out and said
with tears, "Lord, I believe; help my unbelief!"*

MARK 9:24 NKJV

• •

Entrusting friends and family to God's care isn't always easy. One reason is that as women, we're born caretakers—and we doubt anyone can care for those we love as well as we do. Faith assures us that God is the only perfect caregiver. When we worry about someone, we're doubting God's love, power, and plan for that person's life. Bring every doubt and worry to God in prayer. Allow Him to transform your doubts into faith.

A WRITTEN INVITATION

Ever since the world was created, people have seen the earth and sky. Through everything God made, they can clearly see his invisible qualities—his eternal power and divine nature.

ROMANS 1:20 NLT

God's story is written in more places than the Bible. It's written in the glory of the setting sun, the faithfulness of the ocean tides, the symphony of a thunderstorm, and the detail of a dragonfly's wing. It's written in every cell of you. Take time to "read" more about who God is as described through His creation. Contemplate His organizational skills, creative genius, and love of diversity. Consider nature God's written invitation to worship and wonder.

HALF-BAKED?

*Let patience have its perfect work, that you may
be perfect and complete, lacking nothing.*

JAMES 1:4 NKJV

· ·

There's nothing delicious, delightful, or desirable about a half-baked cake. You have to wait until it's finished baking, no matter how hungry you are or how tight your time constraints may be. Impatience pushes us to take shortcuts and settle for second best. It can also rob us of opportunities to grow in our faith. The next time you feel impatience rising up in you, ask God, "What would You like me to learn while I wait?"

CLOTHE YOUR HEART

*What matters is not your outer appearance—
the styling of your hair, the jewelry you wear, the cut
of your clothes—but your inner disposition.*
1 PETER 3:3–4 MSG

For many women, getting dressed is a bit like painting a portrait. They put themselves together in a way that reflects how they want others to see them. Successful? Confident? Youthful? A bit of a rebel? Who you are inside speaks much louder than what you wear on the outside. As you allow God, through faith, to clothe your heart in love and compassion, you'll automatically become more attractive. You'll draw others toward you and God, regardless of what you have on.

FAITH, HOPE, AND LOVE

Love never fails. . . . And now these three remain:
faith, hope and love. But the greatest of these is love.
1 Corinthians 13:8, 13 niv

· ·

When everything else fades away to nothingness, love will remain. Think about that for a moment. When this earth as we know it is long gone, God's love for us will remain. All our possessions, talents, and abilities will fade, but the way we treated others—the love we showed them—will linger forever in their memories. Love people in such a way that they will remember you long after you're gone.

ERASED!

*When you ask for something, you must have
faith and not doubt. Anyone who doubts is like
an ocean wave tossed around in a storm.*
JAMES 1:6 CEV

. . . .

You wouldn't ask a gardener to trim your hair or a house painter to paint
your nails. When you ask someone to do something, you ask only those
who you believe can actually do what needs done. God can do anything
that's in line with His will. If you pray without expecting God to answer,
doubt is derailing your faith. Ask God to help you understand the "whys"
behind your doubts. He can help you erase each one.

ALWAYS HOPE

Remember, our Lord's patience gives people time to be saved.
2 Peter 3:15 NLT

• •

We're thankful for God's patience with us. He consistently honors us with time to grow, room to fail, and an endless supply of mercy and love. But we aren't the only ones who benefit from His patience. He extends it to everyone, including those we feel are slow learners or those we consider hopeless cases. In God's eyes and in God's timing, there's always hope. Ask God to help you extend to others what He so graciously extends to you.

YOU'RE LOVED

The humble will see their God at work and be glad.
Let all who seek God's help be encouraged.
PSALM 69:32 NLT

. . . .

Asking someone for help can be humbling. Even if that someone is a close friend. But if she agrees to assist you and actually comes through for you, you can't help but be encouraged. Knowing someone reached out to you means that person cares. It means you matter. You're loved. Know that God's help means the very same thing. He cares for you because He cares about you. Let that fact encourage you in your faith today.

GROWING FRIENDSHIP AND FAITH

When we get together, I want to encourage you in your faith, but I also want to be encouraged by yours.

ROMANS 1:12 NLT

When women get together, there's usually a whole lot of talking going on. Conversing, counseling, giggling, and catching up on the latest news are all wonderful ways to build a friendship. But if you want to build your faith, take time to encourage one another. Tell your friends how you've seen God at work in their lives. Share what God's been teaching you. Ask questions. Pray. Praise. Your friendship will grow right along with your faith.

SPIRITUAL ARSENAL

*Put on all the armor that God gives, so you can
defend yourself against the devil's tricks.*
EPHESIANS 6:11 CEV

. . . .

A woman donning armor brings to mind images of Xena the Warrior
Princess or Joan of Arc. But the armor God offers is neither fantasy nor
outdated. It's a spiritual arsenal of offensive and defensive gear. It's
comprised of weapons such as truth, righteousness, peace, and faith.
There's a battle going on every day for your mind and heart. But there's no
reason to be afraid. Through faith, God's given you everything you need
to be victorious.

PATH TO HEAVEN

*God loved the people of this world so much that he
gave his only Son, so that everyone who has faith in
him will have eternal life and never really die.*

JOHN 3:16 CEV

- -

Eternal life doesn't begin after you die. It begins the day you put your faith
in Jesus' love. Right now, you're in the childhood of eternity. You're learning
and growing. Like a toddler trying to master the art of walking, you may
wobble a bit at times. But if you fall, God helps get you back on your feet
again. Once your faith sets you on the path toward heaven, nothing—
absolutely nothing—can prevent you from reaching your destination.

JOURNAL YOUR WAY TO A DEEPER FAITH

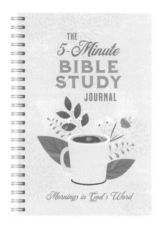

The 5-Minute Bible Study Journal for Women: Mornings in God's Word

In just 5 minutes, you will *Read* (minute 1–2), *Understand* (minute 3), *Apply* (minute 4), and *Pray* (minute 5) God's Word through meaningful, focused, morning Bible study. *The 5-Minute Bible Study Journal for Women: Mornings in God's Word* includes more than 90 Bible studies that will start your day off right and speak to your heart in a powerful way.

Spiral / 978-1-63609-465-6

The Prayer Map for Hope and Healing

This engaging prayer journal is a calming and creative way for you to more fully experience the healing power of prayer in your life. Each page features a lovely 2-color design that guides you to write out specific thoughts, ideas, and lists. . .creating a specific "map" for you to follow as you talk to God.

Spiral / 978-1-63609-424-3

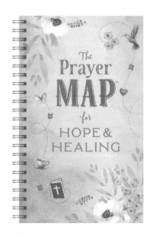